Date _____

This book belongs

_____   -

Given by _____

The Beatitudes for Children

Rosemarie Gortler & Donna Piscitelli
Illustrated by Mimi Sternhagen

Our Sunday Visitor Publishing Division
Our Sunday Visitor, Inc.
Huntington, IN 46750

● ● ●

Nihil Obstat
Rev. Paul F. deLadurantaye
Censor Deputatus

Imprimatur
Rev. Frank J. Ready, Vicar General
Diocese of Arlington
December 22, 2008

The *Nihil Obstat* and *Imprimatur* are official declarations that a book or pamphlet is free of doctrinal or moral error. No implication is contained therein that those who have granted the *Nihil Obstat* and *Imprimatur* agree with the contents, opinions, or statements expressed.

Our Sunday Visitor Publishing Division
Our Sunday Visitor, Inc.
200 Noll Plaza
Huntington, IN 46750

ISBN: 978-1-59276-545-4 (Inventory No. T821)
LCCN: 2008943403

Cover and interior designs by Amanda Miller
Cover and interior art by Mimi Sternhagen

PRINTED IN THE UNITED STATES OF AMERICA

Contents

A Letter From the Authors

Dear Children,

When Jesus was on earth, thousands of people followed Him, and they were eager to hear what He would teach them. One day, He sat down on the side of a mountain to preach a very important sermon. The people following Him sat down, too. Leaning back on their elbows, they waited for Him to speak. The message He preached is called the Sermon on the Mount. The first part of the sermon is the Beatitudes.

Jesus brought us the Beatitudes, which speak of the grace of God and teach us how to love God and one another.

The Beatitudes are eight lessons to help us journey through life as God wants. The first three lessons tell us how to have a deeper relationship with God. The next five lessons tell us how our life will be different because of that deeper relationship.

Each Beatitude begins with the word "Blessed," which means "you are favored by God." Each Beatitude ends with a promise of what we will inherit in heaven. The word "Beatitude" means "abundant happiness." What a promise!

Some of the words Jesus used may sound sad and painful to us today. But that was the language of His time, and the people on the side of the mountain that day understood what Jesus was saying. They knew He was teaching how to live a joyful, God-centered life. When we listen to what these lessons mean in the language of today, we see that the Beatitudes teach about a love that is bigger than anything on earth.

As a matter of fact, Pope Benedict XVI, in his book *Jesus of Nazareth*, speaks of the Beatitudes as a description of Jesus' life!

God bless you.

Rosemarie and Donna

The Beatitudes

"Blessed are the poor in spirit,
     for theirs is the kingdom of heaven.

"Blessed are those who mourn,
     for they will be comforted.

"Blessed are the meek,
     for they will inherit the earth.

"Blessed are those who hunger
     and thirst for righteousness,
          for they will be filled.

"Blessed are the merciful,
     for they will receive mercy.

"Blessed are the pure in heart,
     for they will see God.

"Blessed are the peacemakers,
     for they will be called children of God.

"Blessed are those who are persecuted
     for righteousness' sake,
          for theirs is the kingdom of heaven."

Matthew 5:3-10

Jesus' First Lesson

"Blessed are the poor in spirit, for theirs is the kingdom of heaven."

This teaching of Jesus might sound strange — that God wants us to be poor in spirit. It sounds as though God wants us to have no money, and to be sad, if we want to be with Him in heaven someday.

But that's not what Jesus meant when He spoke of being poor in spirit.

Remember, the words Jesus used have a different meaning in today's world. When Jesus said "*poor in spirit*," He was telling us that we need to be humble and to place **all** our trust in God, knowing that God is always there for us. Jesus wants us to rely on God, to be humble, and to know that all our gifts and talents come from Him. When we trust that God is in charge, we are **humbled** — which means we are "*poor in spirit*."

The people listening to the sermon on the mountain knew that Jesus was teaching them to put their lives in God's hands. His message to them, and to us today, is simple: Talk to God. Trust Him. And tell Him your troubles.

Telling God about our needs, our worries, and our joys shows that we humbly trust Him, and that we believe that everything in our life is important to Him.

We find our true self in our relationship with God. His **promise** is that the kingdom of heaven is ours when we have this humble relationship with Him.

"Come to me, all who labor and are heavy laden, and I will give you rest." (Matthew 11:28)

My Prayer

Dear Father,

Please help me to remember that pride is the opposite of being humble, and that anger and revenge only bring sadness and misery.

Help me to remember that Jesus taught us that being poor in spirit means being humble. Being humble means knowing that we are dependent upon You for our gifts and blessings.

I want my heart to be peaceful. Help me to try to always be grateful and to always lean on You.

Thank You, Father. Amen.

Jesus' Second Lesson

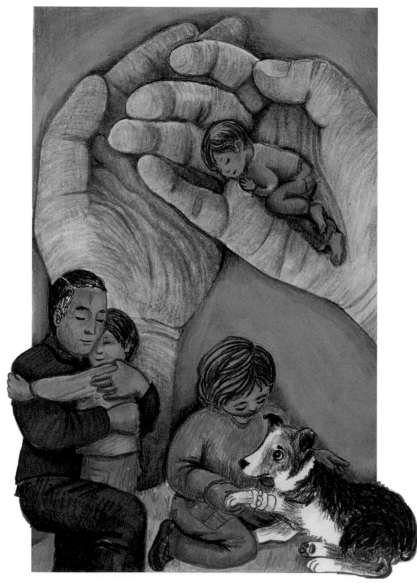

"Blessed are those who mourn, for they will be comforted."

No matter how big you are, God is bigger!

In your mind, picture yourself as curled up and resting in the palms of God's large, warm, loving hands. That's a heavenly picture!

On earth, we sometimes experience sorrow or illness. Maybe we have a friend whose parents are divorced, or perhaps we know someone who has lost a family member or a friend. When we experience sadness in our life, we can better understand the sadness in other people's lives. Sorrowful experiences teach us how to be kind to others and to reach out to those in need. This is called **compassion**.

When we are sad, we look for comfort. We might go to Mom or Dad or to a grandparent or a trusted friend. It is especially comforting to go to the One who loves us so much — God the Father!

Jesus understands how we feel because He experienced the same pain and heartache that we sometimes experience. He knew how it felt to be left out, abandoned, lonely, misunderstood, hated, and rejected. He cried when His friend Lazarus died. His own foster father, Joseph, died during Jesus' lifetime.

Jesus certainly knew physical pain when He was nailed to a cross, after being beaten and tortured. He also knew how it felt to be loved and to be happy, and to be funny and laugh.

During all of Jesus' life, God comforted Him. Even during His greatest agony in Gethsemane, Jesus was comforted by an angel of God.

God comforts us, too. He gives us people in our life who care for us. And from the moment we are born, we have a guardian angel to watch over us!

God also gave us the treasure of the Eucharist. When we receive the real Body and Blood of Jesus, we are intimately close to Him. What a perfect time to tell Him about our troubles and our feelings.

During our life, we ask God for a little of the peace we will one day receive in heaven, when we will be wrapped in His loving embrace.

In this Beatitude, Jesus **promises** that all of our sorrows will be comforted.

What a promise!

Blessed be the God and Father of our Lord Jesus Christ, the Father of mercies and God of all comfort.
(2 Corinthians 1:3)

My Prayer

Dear Father,

When we lose someone we love, we know that You, Father, will comfort us. Remind me to turn to You and to ask for comfort.

When I am sad, or when I hurt, please help me to remember that You always walk ahead of me, and that You are with me.

Thank You, Father. Amen.

Jesus' Third Lesson

"Blessed are the meek, for they will inherit the earth."

The word "meek" usually brings to mind a picture of someone who is weak or wimpy. But when Jesus used the word "meek," He meant that, in serving God, we need to be humble and obedient, and to know that we are powerless (like little children) where God is concerned. After all, we are His children!

When we are humble, we recognize that we can't be a "know-it-all." Humble people know we all need God, and other people, in order to grow and learn. When we are humble and obedient, it's easier to love God, and to love others. There's a bonus in this! Humble people are generally more lovable. It's easy to like humble people.

Think about this: Jesus is God — the Almighty! But when He was on earth, He chose to be very meek and gentle. He always obeyed His Father. Even when He knew He would die on the cross, He accepted His Father's will, even though He knew it would be very painful.

Jesus is our model. He taught us to follow in His footsteps — to listen and to learn from those who love us and guide us in life.

Being obedient isn't always easy. It's often more fun to take the easier path. But think back: we usually get into a lot of trouble when we don't do the right thing, when we are disobedient. Getting into trouble is no fun!

Jesus said the meek will inherit the earth. He never said it would be easy! Being meek takes real effort, such as being nice to others even when we don't feel like it or when we don't like them, or walking away from a fight (when possible), or admitting that we are wrong. All of these things, and more, require humility.

We can always talk to God when the going gets tough and ask Him for help. We need to tell Him how rough it is. The trick is to **know** that He is listening, and that He will find the right way to help — in **His** time. That's real faith and humility. That's the powerlessness He was talking about when He said, "Blessed are the meek."

When we are meek, we understand that we have much to learn. But God will give us everything we need. And the **promise** is that we will inherit the earth.

With righteousness he shall
judge the poor, and decide with equity
for the meek of the earth.
(Isaiah 11:4)

My Prayer

Dear Father,

I don't really like the words "obey" and "obedience."
But I know that when I do what I'm told to do by
the people who love me, my life is easier, and I don't
make a mess of things.

I know that You love me more than I can ever, ever
really know. Please help me to do Your will. I really
want to obey Your commandments. I want to be the
kind and gentle person that Jesus said would inherit
the earth. But sometimes it's so hard, and I get so
tempted to do what I really know is wrong. Please
help me to try harder when this happens.

Thank You, Father. Amen.

Jesus' Fourth Lesson

"Blessed are those who hunger and thirst for righteousness, for they will be filled."

Many of the people had walked a long way to hear Jesus teach. The wind had blown sand at them, stinging their faces. So they had to wrap their faces in cloth and turn their heads against this painful wind. But they still wanted to listen to Jesus.

Now they were tired, hot, hungry, and thirsty. There were no drinking fountains or restaurants. They felt sick from hunger and thirst!

Did you ever miss a meal or feel very thirsty? In this Beatitude, Jesus is asking if we want righteousness as much as a starving person wants food or a very thirsty person needs water. What did Jesus mean by "righteousness?"

Righteousness has four points:

1. Doing the very best we can do in everything. This teaches us to put our best foot forward at all times.

2. Trying to be the best person we can be.

3. Wanting to do what is right at all times, and standing up for what it right.

4. Wanting what is right for others. This requires us to be cheerleaders for others, to assist those who need help, and sometimes to put others before ourselves.

This seems simple, doesn't it?

It isn't always simple, because we are often tempted to follow the crowd. But when we live this Beatitude, we discover that our relationship with God means more than anything else! We try to live the way God wants us to live, to follow His rules, and to do His will.

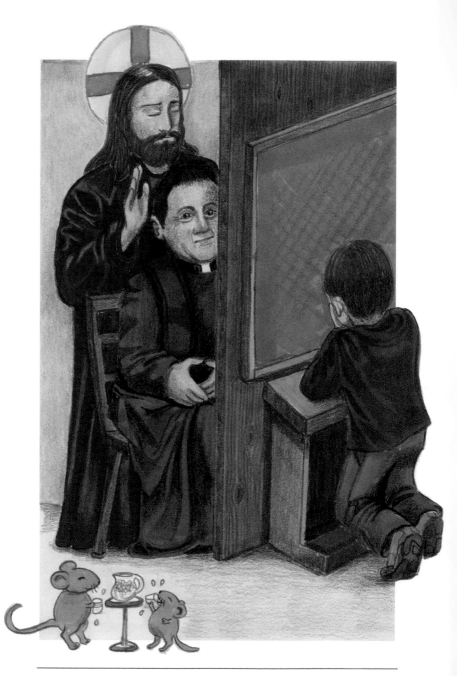

And if we make a mistake, we try again. We ask our God for His forgiveness, and He fills us with His love.

When we seek righteousness, Jesus *promises* that we will be satisfied — just as we are satisfied when we are hungry and thirsty and then someone gives us food and drink!

Where sin increased, grace abounded all the more, so that, as sin reigned in death, grace also might reign through righteousness to eternal life through Jesus Christ our Lord. (Romans 5:20-21)

My Prayer

Dear Father,

I need help to really want to do the right thing. I know that sometimes I make excuses when I sin, and sometimes it is so hard not to follow the crowd.

I need Your help. Please speak to me when I think of doing wrong. Let me hear Your will for me. You know how easy it is for me to make excuses. I really need You to help me to always want to live according to Your word.

Thank You, Father. Amen.

Jesus' Fifth Lesson

"Blessed are the merciful, for they will receive mercy."

God's mercy is like heaven. It is infinite. God is all-forgiving because He loves us. He asks us to be forgiving and merciful toward others.

What does it mean to be merciful? Being merciful is being charitable, generous, compassionate, and patient toward others. It means showing kindness and love to others, especially those who are weak.

Blessed Mother Teresa was compassionate. She devoted her life to helping the poor, the sick, and the dying. The people she helped in India were considered "the untouchables." They were the people no one else would help.

Mother Teresa said that she wouldn't do this work for a million dollars — but she did do it for love of Jesus and His people! She had a merciful and compassionate heart. Only with God's love could she love others enough to care for the sick and the dying as she did.

Mother Teresa lived this Beatitude!

God wants us to be loving and merciful toward others, just as He is loving and merciful toward us. Jesus gave us the **Lord's Prayer**. In this prayer, He explained one way to be merciful:

> *"And forgive us our trespasses,*
> *As we forgive those who trespass against us."*
> *(Matthew 6:12)*

In this prayer, we ask God to teach us to forgive as He forgives, even as we ask Him for His forgiveness and mercy.

God understands how much we need His mercy.

When we are merciful to others, God **promises** mercy to us.

> *For judgment is without mercy to*
> *one who has shown no mercy; yet*
> *mercy triumphs over judgment.*
> *(James 2:13)*

Our Father who art in hea
Hallowed be thy name. Thy k
come, thy will be earth
is in heaven. Giv day
daily bread and our t
as we ss a
And lead tion
deliver us

My Prayer

Dear Father,

I say the prayer that Jesus taught — "Our Father who art in heaven ..." — **almost** every day. But often I don't think about what the words mean. When I pay attention to the words, I understand that I am supposed to praise You, obey You, and always trust You. I know that You want me to forgive others when they hurt me, and to pray for Your help.

I don't always do these things. Sometimes I try to get back at others for hurting me. I want to be better.

I need Your help to remind me to care about others. Please help me to grow in patience, kindness, and compassion. Help me to live my faith and to trust You.

Thank You, Father. Amen.

Jesus' Sixth Lesson

"Blessed are the pure in heart, for they will see God."

Pure in heart? Always? How is that possible?

To understand this Beatitude, it is helpful to look at the lives of the saints.

St. Joseph is one who is considered to be pure in heart. God wanted Joseph to raise and protect His Son, Jesus, and to care for and protect the mother of His Son, Mary.

This was a huge task. Joseph, Mary, and Jesus lived in dangerous times. When Joseph took Mary as his wife, he knew that she had promised to remain a virgin. Joseph did all that God asked him to do, free of selfish intentions. His motives were pure. This is why we describe St. Joseph as "***pure in heart***."

So how can we be pure in heart? God hasn't asked us to be exactly like Joseph. He asks us to strive to do the right thing for the right reasons. This means living our lives without always seeking personal gain.

This is difficult in our world. Television, the Internet, and the messages of this world tell us to put our own needs first. They tell us that we have to have a beautiful body, lots of friends, and plenty of money to be happy. Having these things is not bad, but they are **gifts** from God. Being pure in heart does not mean we can't work to have these things. It does mean that we are thankful for God's gifts, and that we recognize that living according to God's word is more important than anything else.

Being pure in heart also means practicing acts of charity — sometimes putting the **needs** of others before our **wants**. Jesus said that the first will be last and the last will be first. He taught us that when we put our own needs after the needs of others, we will be rewarded in heaven.

Pure and selfless acts are very difficult to do, but they bring true happiness. Jesus teaches us to examine our own motives in what we say and do.

The pure in heart will see God. This is the **promise** of this Beatitude. What a promise — to actually see God!

> **Truly God is good to the upright,**
> **to those who are pure in heart.**
> **(Psalms 73:1)**

My Prayer

Dear Father,

Please help me to **want** to be kind to others without always thinking of myself. Help me to do good things for others even if it means going out of my way when I don't feel like it. I want to do things because of my love for You, but I sometimes get kind of selfish.

I would like Your help to stop making excuses for being this way. I know I can be better.

Please help me, Father, to make better choices, and to have a charitable heart.

Thank You, Father. Amen.

Jesus' Seventh Lesson

"Blessed are the peacemakers, for they will be called children of God."

Jesus said, "Peace I leave with you; my peace I give to you" (John 14:27). In Jesus' language, the word "peace" means being in the presence of God, and doing God's work.

A peacemaker may or may not be the same thing as a peace lover. Sometimes we think that the true peacemaker is the one who will keep quiet and not make waves when he or she sees wrong happening, for fear that speaking up will cause trouble. That is a peace lover. The peacemaker will try to correct what is wrong.

When Jesus was on earth, He was a peacemaker. He lived a humble life. He loved the poor, the lepers, and the sinners. He treated all people as children of God, and He taught that a person's station in life did not determine his or her place in heaven. Jesus always looked for social justice.

In our own life, we often see injustices — things happening that aren't right. What is the peacemaker called to do?

Peacemakers identify wrong. Sometimes they can safely speak out against these wrongs. Sometimes all they can do is report the wrong to someone in authority. **Most important**, peacemakers don't join in the wrongdoing. This can be very difficult, because it is sometimes easier to follow the crowd, or to just turn away.

So what does a peacemaker do when faced with a difficult situation? Being a peacemaker means doing whatever you can **safely** do to change a bad situation. Jesus wants us to love everyone, even those who do wrong. He wants us to be nice to them. It's possible to do the right thing without accepting wrong behavior.

We have to ask God's help to do this, because we need His grace to see the truth, and to have the strength to act on His truth.

Jesus **promises** that as peacemakers we will be called the **children of God**.

"Peace be with you."
(John 20:19)

My Prayer

Dear Father,

I really do know right from wrong, and yet I sometimes don't bother to say or do anything when kids are being mean to other kids. I don't want to get involved because I want to be cool.

Jesus wants me to be a peacemaker. Please give me the courage to safely do or say the right thing to help someone who is being picked on. If I cannot do this safely, please give me the courage to say something to a teacher or a parent who can be a peacemaker.

Help me to look for the good in others.

Thank You, Father. Amen.

Jesus' Eighth Lesson

PHILOMENA

TAR-
CISIUS
+
JOAN
OF ARC

MAXI-
MILIAN
KOLBE

THOMAS MORE

"Blessed are those who are persecuted for righteousness' sake, for theirs is the kingdom of heaven."

What is persecution? Christ was persecuted when He was crucified on the cross. The early Christians were persecuted and killed because they believed in Christ.

It's awesome to think about Christians who were persecuted throughout the centuries and how they made it possible for us to practice our faith today.

It is amazing to think about how Christ, who is God, allowed Himself to be crucified. He did not yell at or threaten those who persecuted Him. He suffered for **us**. And He showed us how He wants us to bear suffering for Him.

Sometimes in our daily lives we are persecuted. If we try to follow God's commandments, people might make fun of us. If we pray in public, or profess a belief in God, or are kind to someone that others do not like, some people might poke fun at us. This is persecution for righteous behavior.

Jesus wants us to be meek, and to respond to this kind of persecution with loving kindness — but we should never reject Him or say we don't believe in Him.

Standing up for Christ is the right thing to do.

There are small ways to do this every day. Asking the Holy Spirit to help you recall information before taking a test is recognizing the power of God (however, only if you studied and learned the information to begin with!). Reading about and studying your faith is standing up for God. Living your faith is also standing up for God. Being charitable to others is doing God's work.

If we stand up for what God teaches, we are **promised** the kingdom of heaven!

Blessed are they who observe justice,
who do righteousness at all times!
(Psalms 106:3)

My Prayer

Dear Father,

I am a Christian, so I know how important it is to praise You every day, and to give You thanks for all my blessings.

Sometimes I need some help to remember to take at least one minute every day to praise You, to thank You for meals, and to give You thanks for all of the other big and little blessings You give to me. Also, if I forget, please remind me to take just one more minute at 3 o'clock every afternoon to thank Jesus for the sacrifice He made for me on the cross.

And please, Father, help me not to hide the fact that I am a Christian.

Thank You, Father. Amen.

For Family Discussion

Jesus taught us the Beatitudes a long time ago just to show us how we can choose to be blessed. He began every Beatitude with the word "Blessed." To be "blessed" means to enjoy great happiness, great delight, and great joy! The Ten Commandments give us the "rules," and the Eight Beatitudes tell us how to interpret and follow those rules.

Jesus sat on the side of that mountain to explain to us that being blessed is to know God's peace — to have a wonderful relationship with our God. In the Beatitudes, Jesus explains **ALL** of life's experiences. There is no life experience that is not addressed by the Beatitudes. They make up a living map, directing us on our journey to eventually be with our God

Jesus came to us so that we might have life abundantly. The Beatitudes teach us to recognize our need for God, and the need to respect, love, and care for one another. The Beatitudes are all concerned with virtue: to love and to be loved; to feel secure during times of mourning; to be able to forgive and be forgiven; and in the end, to be blessed with all the joy He promised.

Think about it! What a great lesson to teach children. If we try to follow His map, we won't be sorry — we'll be blessed!

Please check out "Be-Attitudes For Family Discussion" online at **www.osv.com** — go to "BOOKS" and select "Book Resources and Downloads." We hope your family will have lively discussions about the Be-Attitudes!

About the Authors

Rosemarie Gortler is an R.N. and a licensed professional counselor. She is also an extraordinary minister of the Eucharist, a member of the Secular Franciscan Order, and a volunteer for Project Rachel. Rosemarie and her husband, Fred, have five children and nineteen grandchildren.

Donna Piscitelli is a school administrator in Fairfax, Virginia. She is active in her church and in Christian outreach. She and her husband, Stephen, have four children and ten grandchildren.

Mimi Sternhagen is a home-school teacher and mother of five children. She and her husband, Don, assist with Family Life ministry in their parish. In addition to her collaborated works with Rosemarie and Donna, Mimi has illustrated *Catholic Cardlinks: Patron Saints* and *Teach Me About Mary*.

The authors extend their gratitude to Father Donald Rooney of St. Mary of the Immaculate Conception Catholic Church in Fredericksburg, Virginia, for his assistance in the preparation of this book. They also extend a special thank you to their husbands, Fred Gortler and Steve Piscitelli, for their loving support during the writing of this entire series.

Other books in this series include:

Just Like Mary

Little Acts of Grace

Living the 10 Commandments for Children

The Mass Book for Children